HAIKU
TRADITIONS

by

LEON TEFFT

Haiku Traditions

FIRST EDITION

ISBN: 979-8-9910818-0-1

Written and edited by Leon Tefft

LEONTEFFT.COM

CONTENTS

For my wife, Hollie

forever in my heart
therefore
forever in my words

Introduction

Thank you, dear reader, for purchasing my book. Your support and interest mean the world to me.

I've been captivated by haiku for almost half a century, reading, studying and writing through my travels. Haiku has taught me ways of observing and interacting with the world around me that I never would have known otherwise. It always impresses me how three short lines of words can pack as much punch as a well-written haiku. And yet, within such simplicity lie incredible layers of nuance and complexity.

When I set out to write this book, I was determined to make it one readers would want to buy, read and display in their bookcases—one they could revisit to contemplate poems further to derive their meanings. It is not just a book of poems but a book to expand thinking and observe the world in new ways, as I've learned, to help put readers in touch with their essence of being. This book is a tool for personal growth and self-discovery, a journey through the beauty and complexity of life, as seen through the lens of haiku and other short-form poetry. I hope it will serve as a guide and companion on your own journey of self-discovery.

I also ensured you would get plenty of bang for your buck with this book. Poetry book authors can be vague in specifying the content of their books. I've often found books (not chapbooks, mind you) with fewer than 100 haiku, even some with less than 50 pages, with one haiku printed per page. That's fine if you're short on time, but different from what I consider worth the price of admission.

What distinguishes this book is the quantity of poems and the quality and diversity of the forms included. This book contains 300 original poems, each thoughtfully written. Among these, you'll find 220 haiku, 40 senryu, 30 tanka and 10 haibun, each offering a unique perspective and style of writing. I did not sacrifice quality for quantity.

The book's title, *Traditions*, refers to the writing style where I began—the traditional 5-7-5 syllable pattern for English haiku and senryu. Following suit, tanka included here similarly adhere to a 5-7-5-7-7 syllable pattern. This book honors the form that most people become familiar with when they first learn about haiku. The poetry in this book should prove accessible and entertaining for all.

Each of these 300 poems is a unique opportunity for contemplation. All are carefully written and have something to offer. The meaning you derive from each one is entirely up to you. As you read, I encourage you to reflect on your experiences, feelings and thoughts and see how they resonate with the words on the page. Ultimately, I hope you find unexpected insights and take away something more from my poetry than you expected.

I invite you to share your thoughts and interpretations of the poems, as poetry is a conversation, a dialogue between the poet and the reader. You can connect with me through my author website at LEONTEFFT.COM.

SECTION I
HAIKU

What is Haiku?

Haiku, a poetic form that traces its origins to 13th-century Japan, was initially used as the opening phrase in long-form renga poetry. During Japan's Edo Period in the 16th century, renowned masters of the form, including Matsuo Basho (1644-1694), Yosa Buson (1716-1784) and Kobayashi Issa (1763-1828), practiced the standalone haiku, initially known as *hokku*. By the 19th century, hokku had evolved into the current form known as haiku. While traditional haiku poets focused on nature and seasonal elements, contemporary haiku poets can explore any subject.

Haiku, at its core, is a simple yet profound form of poetry that anyone can readily try their hand at. My introduction to haiku came during high school in a creative writing class. My teacher taught me the same information that most people likely learn when they first discover haiku, which distills into two basic rules:

1.   haiku comprises three lines that do not need to rhyme
2.   haiku adheres to a 5-7-5 syllable count pattern

Virtually everyone familiar with haiku is aware of these two "rules." However, when discussing syllables, that rule, in partic-ular, is a point of contention among many haiku writers.

The Rule of Syllables

The 5-7-5 syllable pattern, or 17-syllable count, is based on the Japanese *on*, which refers to phonetic units arranged in a haiku but are not identical to syllables. When translated to another language from Japanese, the *on* of the haiku typically will not match the new language form in syllables—likewise, writing a 17-syllable haiku in English, for example, and translating it to Japanese results in a version that will probably have many more *on* than desired.

Because syllable counts can differ significantly across languages during translation, many poets disregard the traditional haiku rule of 17 syllables in a 5-7-5 pattern. Some poets think of the syllable rule as a silly grade school-level way of composing haiku, while others find it challenging to write an effective haiku while adhering to a rigid form. I see valid points on both sides of this subject.

As I've delved deeper into the study and practice of haiku, I've deviated from the traditional syllable rule in favor of a more concise and elegant haiku composition. However, for this book, I've chosen to honor the form I first learned and the one with which most readers will be familiar. The haiku, senryu and tanka here follow their traditionally learned English syllable count forms, hence the title, *Traditions*.

The true power of haiku lies in its ability to evoke strong impressions with just a few carefully chosen words. A well-crafted haiku captures a fleeting moment in the present tense and delivers it with clarity and conciseness. Reading a haiku should feel like a seamless stream of consciousness, conveying a sense of "being there" in the moment. A well-crafted haiku should showcase the poet's skill in weaving its elements together regardless of how many syllables it has.

A Word on Grammar

In the spirit of brevity and capturing the flow of a moment in time with simplicity, haiku are typically written without capitalization and punctuation. It is often a matter of preference for poets to choose if and when they capitalize words or add punctuation to their haiku. For instance, I always capitalize some words, such as the word "I," proper names and holidays. They don't look or feel right to me otherwise.

Punctuation can be trickier. Some haiku poets disdain punctuation of any kind, feeling that if a phrase needs punctuation to illustrate a break or prevent the haiku from sounding like a run-on sentence, it should be rewritten not to require it. I agree; however, if I feel an em dash or ellipsis enhances the feel of a haiku, I will use it. I also find that exclamation points and question marks are often necessary for specific usages. I always address these on a case-by-case basis.

As a general practice, one should become familiar with reading and composing haiku in lowercase and without punctuation since this approach aligns with the form's innate simplicity and immediacy.

And Here We Go

I've just scratched the surface of haiku's form, aiming to provide casual readers with a solid foundation for better understanding its structure and objectives and what to be aware of when reading these poems. If you expand your study, you'll find many different styles and interpretations of haiku. For this book, though, I have provided the information necessary to turn through these pages to extract the most from these poems.

I recommend that readers give each haiku time to reflect on and contemplate any meaning received from it before moving on to the next one.

The Haiku Section includes five chapters: Spring, Summer, Autumn, Winter and Modern. I have written these poems with my preference for minimal capitalization and punctuation.

Thank you for reading, and please enjoy.

SPRING
HAIKU

creeks ferry fables

tales adrift on racing waves

—silence, then fury

greenery ascends

blaze orange and red riot

rest in wan repose

seasons paint portraits

of dreams coloring senses

rapture the canvas

creeping charlie crawls
and wild violet thickens
mice lost in a maze

lemon chamomile
aroma tempting taste buds
sultry steamy sips

white lilac whispers
becalm sleepy green meadows
florid dreams blossom

joyful showers pop
cherry blossom confetti
spring celebration

butterfly orchids
pressed in diary pages
fairy tales to tell

air supremacy—
an aerial fandango
of fierce cardinals[1]

windblown poppy field
brushed in supple scarlet waves
red-tailed hawk circles

wisteria vines
crowning garden pergola
heavenly blue rain

frantic squeaks chipping
at freedom mere pecks away—
duckling emerges

scaling a hilltop
glimpsing majestic mountains
out of breath...breathless

sunrise scenes painted
on skylight panoramas
nature the artist

bright moon decked in clouds
raining drops of silver glow
moonlight wets my face

bumblebees rhyming
daffodil trumpet sonnets
honeyed poetry

cottage birdhouse hung
in the backyard maple tree
new nuthatch neighbors

cherry blossom soap
bubbles on my scented hands
hints of Mount Fuji

hands touch twisted roots
of the oak tree's ageless reach
...to know an old friend[2]

crimson drops of spring
tangled in frozen north winds
icy bleeding hearts

blackthorn wanderer
songs of finches and thrushes
snug in their haven

lonesome daily stroll
to the sycamore tree bench
birdseed for good friends

green white-eye warbler
clashing with cherry blossoms
colorful contrast

zigzagging boardwalk
navigates spring dogwood trees
koi splash in the pond

spring looks with jade eyes
at melting snow and blue sky
tulips spring to life

orchids serenade
warm orange blossom breezes
ambrosial song

wood chipper chatters
through desolate forest trees
creek frogs in the midst

springing grasslands
revive slumbering landscapes
early birds touch down

vanquisher reborn
sun's glory treads broken shards
of conquered midnights

picturesque meadow
silk breezes moving tulips
tulips moving me

spirited young birds
rollicking through woodland trees
eager to partake

coyotes hold forth
ebb and flow of barks and howls
forewarning the night

calm stillness reclaimed
where iron steeds once thundered
nature reigns supreme

snapped twig teetering

between two forked branches

acrobat finch lands

silvereyes roosting

a cherry blossom fanfare

greeting arrivals

deer navigate

oceans of golden rapeseed

seeking safe harbor

tsunami lanterns—
for candles doused by darkness
flames burn forevermore

unstoppable force
meets immovable object
blue jay swoops a crow

mute swan and cygnet
traversing verdant cattails
early swim lesson

whisper of warm air
on dew-covered maple leaves
the forest rises

Endnotes

1. First published in *Cold Moon Journal*—April 2024.
2. This haiku was inspired by the iconic beech Medusa Tree in downtown Greenville, South Carolina.

SUMMER
HAIKU

darkness severs dusk
stardust bleeds in the night sky
sleep to dream again

poignant red roses
remembrance of what is lost
before the next bloom[1]

dandelion crown
beams aristocratic pride
a weed nonetheless

oars thrust the canoe
to a silent sandy shore
herons guide the way

sunny dahlias
glamorize lonesome meadows
—any shade but black

crimson rose dappled
with shimmering sunrise dew
eager aphids flock

eyeing a dark cave
too dire to calmly venture
bats fly unhindered

windswept summer clouds
sketch a mother's gentle face
whispered lullabies

poppies catch rays
softly on lustrous petals
scarlet fantasy

muskmelon incense

honeyed satin smoke fragrance

quenches karmic bliss

seafront promenade

gooey banana taffy

stuck to my sneakers

blueberry pancake

and orange mimosa brunch

smiles cross our table

supple hammock sways
under breezy island palms
dream and dream again

dreamy chiffon skies
paint a pastel dusk vignette
fireflies reignite

vermilion stained sky
mocking blood pacts spilled in dust
desert song dogs howl

fiery dragonfly
flashing kaleidoscope wings
—epiphany stirs

rocket red starlight
vanilla dollop sugar cones
drizzle happy hands

childhood memories
rush through castles carved in sand
wrinkles map my skin

spinning world racing
through a speeding galaxy
inchworm bides its time

cozy campfire s'mores
dusted with moonlight magic
sticky sweet fingers

tenacious vultures
cocksure in their grisly task
—I steer to the left

tempting red dragon
radiating fruity scents
Venus traps her fly

elegant endgame
chased by the caterpillar
stunning butterfly

rusted wagon wheel
sunk in country meadow soil
shade for katydids

lumps of crushed sugar
stirred in crystal clear water
hummingbird heaven

tumbleweeds roving
through cities that never were
views never enjoyed[2]

white sweet alyssum
snowdrifts carpet the garden
summer masquerade

bonfire festival—
burning of the winter witch
heralds summer's dawn[3]

lavender ice cream—
velvety summer fragrance
on a dessert dish

tropical resort
champagne and caviar brunch
salt fish past the fence

candlelight lantern
casting stories on the pond
frogs croak in reply

astronomical
heist on a galactic scale
Luna steals the sun

boarding the sailboat
whistling a jolly shanty
—changes in the wind

desert oasis
of tangible delusion
sands through scorched fingers

peeling an orange—
supernova citrus mist
oozing zesty tang

torn from the night sky
sparkling in heavenly eyes
stars shine brighter still

cherry tree orchard
bursting with ripe juicy fruit
sweet summer windfall

hummingbird feeder
hung on the crepe myrtle tree
summer oasis[4]

vine-covered limestone
orange honeysuckle walls
fragrance waterfall

fresh picked salad bowl
everything but radishes
left behind to grow

Endnotes

1. First published in *Petals of Haiku: An Anthology* by Literary Revelations / Gabriela Marie Milton—May 2024.
2. First published in *Cold Moon Journal*—April 2024.
3. Inspired by the Fyr Bal Festival held every June in Door County, Wisconsin.
4. "Crepe myrtle" or "crape myrtle?" Both spellings are correct. I opted for the more common Southern United States spelling since that is where my crepe myrtles are.

AUTUMN
HAIKU

tranquil autumn mist
sunrise nudges weary night
breathing serene peace

frosty maple leaves
crackle in whispering winds
sun-kissed harmonies[1]

treasure of nature's
bountiful autumn harvest
ebbed in wintry rot

clever blackbird caws
sardonic peals of omen
—better watch your step

summer gnats whirling
blithely into autumn chill
nuisance no longer

whistle, hoot and coo—
intellectual wisdom
from the wise old owl

succulent apples
weighing on ripened branches
luscious every bite

marigold and mums
sunflowers and harvest corn
toothy pumpkins grin

belfry clangs herald
all hallows eve witching hour
—I step smartly home

urban squirrels trek
where country squirrels retreat
...missing the city

flashlight beam intrudes
deep into soundless woods
so many eyes glow

black witch weathervane
darting on her iron broom
flying nowhere fast

crystalline dewdrops
beaded on pansy petals
sparkling water dance

driving moonlit roads
amid soaring cornstalk fields
scarecrows watching me

squirrels digging holes
stashing acorns for winter
oak trees not to be

geese drift across ponds
slipping through rushes and reeds
gosling hide-and-seek

red leaf cluttered path
stretching to an orange lake
nothing green in sight

sweet white rice steaming
in a plain porcelain bowl
simple perfection

twilight reflections
sharpened on the mirror lake
someone there sees mine

brandywine leaf scene
sketched on cerulean skies
unsigned masterpiece

cedar butter churn
outside the Amish pole barn
circling cats meow

glimmering twilight
past the chiminea smoke
eyelids weigh heavy

windswept swaying of
sunflowers and bumblebees
sweet autumn tango

Indian summer—
one last precious gasp before
drowning in winter

soaring majesty
looms in a tiny prison
an acorn's patience

hot tea sipped lakeside
in teak adirondack chairs
steam blends morning mist

astral autumn night
Orion chases Virgo
cosmic love affair

nightmarish gargoyles
menacing old mansion walls
ravens pay no mind

aroma of red
scents of yellow and orange
autumn paints the air

chestnuts bounce and roll
past bounding city squirrels
winter provisions

misty sunrise path
beyond the red maple tree
winter lies ahead

unhurried footfalls
waken sleepy forest trails
squirrels pirouette

two deer in season
grand antlers immense with age
—they know the exit

little library
by the oak tree down the street
big worlds in small books

two leaves lingering
on the barren sweetgum tree
welcome overstayed

chrysanthemum sun
raptures blue skies
a chipmunk's ken

hot creekside coffee
savoring the scenery
one sip at a time

smoldering campfire
shadowed by looming mountains
unrequited love

silent deer drifting
charily through barren trees
I watch motionless

butterflies prancing
among falling orange leaves
fall evanescence

Endnotes

1. First published in *Petals of Haiku: An Anthology* by Literary Revelations / Gabriela Marie Milton—May 2024.

WINTER
HAIKU

calm woodlands cradle

delights of muted snowfalls

exquisite silence[1]

pastels drape the sky

across sleepy winter trees

cold embraces night

winter moon revels

in the starry shadow sky

timeless acquaintance

flames writhe with delight
smoke dance and ember fury
flaunting winter's night

brittle branches tremble
beneath white-capped majesty
snowy owl ponders

streams filter remnants
of winter's waning grandeur
fish roam nonchalant

lachrymose winter
adorns cascading waters
teardrop souvenirs

nebulous fox coiled
in a snowdrift oasis
weary yet watching

borealis sky
captivates awestruck wonder
spellbound in beauty

sweet jasmine breezes
await spring's crowning glory
winter yet prevails

crackling jigsaw ice
covers a sun-splashed mill pond
days growing longer

perilous aspens
choke a wavy alpine trail
snow sleds rocket by

piña coladas
sipped seaside under palm trees
glum winter daydream

peculiar warm air
applauds a wintertime day
robins are doubtful

hours bleed to minutes
drain to seconds unending
wolf moon howls tonight

icicle tears drip

prayers on solemn snowdrops

winter exodus

gray winter grove trees

tombstones of bygone seasons

signposts for springtime

virgin powder snow

laid across enticing slopes

skis anxious to carve

flowers of heaven—
in every fallen snowflake
infinity blooms

footprints pressed in snow
vanishing through icy pines
I join the unknown

kneeling by snowdrops
chilling my hands on your headstone
all grieving the dead

carolers crooning
with a chorus of snowmen
warm cheer every year

hot mulled brandy wine
spicy with fruit and honey
luscious potpourri

frosted church windows
glazed with prayers of worship
winter piety

leaden orange dusk
somber on a rainy day
greenery dreaming

fog chases to claim
exiles of winter's domain
only I remain

our cherished park bench
one rose for my one true love
spring has gone away

snow moon wanderer
illumining sapphire skies
silence my shadow

pine cones and berries
ornate baubles dressed in snow
every tree Noel

warmth impervious
to winter's bitterest bite
merry jubilance

blooming cyclamen
splashes of purple and pink
on snow white canvas

purple crocus blooms
dance in snowbound solitude
early burst of spring

soft cinnamon leaves
rustling on a beech tree branch
the wren sings for snow

snow covers bare trees
rusty oak leaves and bluebirds
coloring the storm

alpine theatre
snowy pine tree audience
myself center stage

doorbell sings music
to boots clapping off wet snow
visit of good friends

two strangers searching
for a New Year's midnight kiss—
two strangers no more

first mountain sunrise
lifts through ponderosa pines
stirring sign of hope

twelve grapes at midnight
keeping time as the clock strikes
good fortune to come

sweet mistletoe dreams
hidden under a pillow
for those yet to love

Endnotes

1. First published in *Petals of Haiku: An Anthology* by Literary Revelations / Gabriela Marie Milton—May 2024.

MODERN HAIKU

alluring facade
elegance for your pleasure
a masked hollow soul

loathsome wanderer
fate whispers its dark secret
cold touch of mercy

with threads of chaos
sorrow weaves a tapestry
futile hope of peace

majestic Montblanc

elegant ink flourishes

ecru parchment sings

drawn to decadence

gray seas yield to velvet ropes

forgetful faces[1]

forks in traveled roads

damnable choices in haste

I have my regrets

lies and betrayal

pave grim pathways to hatred

darkest hours emerge

ultimate sinner

blasphemer beyond repent

human just the same

oak wood, bronze and skin

mortal hands, immortal sounds

otherworldly[2]

ribbons bind mountains
with wretched brick and mortar
fellowships broken

cast in the abyss
each day a lost memory
time drags you under

pink lipstick disguise
daily veneer melts away
ritual demise

schemes of naive youth

come undone through jaded years

time hastens anguish[3]

devilish beauty

vexing with venomous charm

motives concealed

all is not conquered

heavenly essence revels

hope triumphs despair

among God's wishes

gracious light shines on bright minds

valor greets the stars[4]

love not gone, but lost

she haunts me even in dreams

elusive mirage

screams shatter dead calm

fangs hunger for burning flesh

blood moon paints the night

sirens vex dark minds
unraveling spellbound dreams
divine hell awaits

bitter hopes decay
entombed in fallen dreams
fate drives iron nails

promise of true love
or remedy for heartbreak
—she proposed neither

rusted anchor soul
dragged across shards of regret
salvation a myth

angel seductions
demigods and charlatans
poison purity

transcendent spirits
exit material worlds
immortality

all my stormy days
I forget the fallen rain
when love pours on me

notions of romance
inflaming a schoolboy crush
torment of young lust

gazing far too long
at her empty merlot glass
red lipstick traces

bittersweet dancing
humming our favorite tune
awkwardly alone

angels among us
imperfect in human form
diamonds in the rough

freight train rolling slow
through dusty desolate towns
vacant horn echoes

pulled curtain faces
crawling the asphalt frontier
muted screams dissolve

stereo needle
grooving a favorite song
three-minute escape

grease paint, guillotines
leopard spot boots and boas
a man called Alice[5]

seduced by your taste
lips craving without protest
morning cappuccino

my friend, my lover
back home to my everything
—a note there waiting

lightning stilettos
striking the concrete jungle
electrifying

small town theatre
with big dreams gracing the stage
Broadway on Main Street

pink lipstick smudges
dirtying a torn collar
secret rendezvous

hands grievous with age
cradle roses close to heart
never too late for love

puritan dogma

raged flames of hysteria

still there are witches

absurdly garish

harlequin prankster of puns

the joker is wild

magical whimsy

sprinkled in stardust-spun words

—a haiku for you

highway to nowhere
writing daydream diaries—
time to turn the page

gardens of eden
grown from naive fantasy
a fool's paradise

spirit from within
not merely paranormal
but purely divine

señorita soars

through dreams across the dance floor

bird of paradise

poetry and prose

freedom from mortal discord

parole for the soul

interchangeable

agony and ecstasy

random whims of love

mad flight of fancy
spun off a carousel dream
lovestruck...out of luck

ruthless time intrudes
on fading fond memories
forgotten gravestones

iceberg dead ahead
rough seas in a leaky boat
same old fight again

baby steps at first
destiny discards darkness
for light to emerge

big city satire
chauffeur's eyes in the mirror
so lost in the crowd

painted clown face smile
masking the artist within
tears betray fiction

dark ruby red lips
amber eyes and diamond rings
jewels of my love

elegant spiral
feathers torn from angel wings
when love dies forlorn

swimming for a key
chained to an iron anchor
unrequited love

feeder of ravens

calling card the ace of spades

dealing early graves

amidst twilight's glow

angel halos encircle

ethereal dreams

intrepid tall ships

restless for bold adventure

chancing the unknown

Endnotes

1. A reference to the velvet ropes of New York's legendary Studio 54 and Steve Rubell's notorious penchant for not allowing the "gray people" to enter the disco.
2. An homage to Rush drummer Neil Peart (1952-2020).
3. First published in *Petals of Haiku: An Anthology* by Literary Revelations / Gabriela Marie Milton—May 2024.
4. Written after the first SpaceX test flight of *Starship*.
5. Alice Cooper, of course.

SECTION II
SENRYU

*"A little song, a little dance
a little seltzer down your pants."*

—Chuckles the Clown / The Mary Tyler Moore Show

If you've gotten the hang of haiku, there's little more to know about understanding senryu. Both share the same form, structure and guidelines for capitalization and punctuation. Where they differ is in the subject matter.

While haiku are usually about nature, senryu are about human nature. Often, senryu include a clever twist of irony, a dash of cynicism, or, more often than not, a blast of comedy. Think of senryu as the haiku version of a pie in the face.

And that's all there is to it.

In the following senryu, I hope you'll discover a thought or two that stimulates your mind and perhaps a few chuckles along the way.

I'm shipwrecked on Mars
water scarce, oxygen low
...oh, but what a view!

threat of certain death
imminent disaster looms
—time for a selfie!

foraging offbeat
anecdotes to write a joke
can't find a punch line

ninja swarm the house
in a silent cloud of doom
golden wags her tail

bulls charge with fury
bears sharpen their dagger claws
where's all my money?!

eating more and more
weight decreasing more and more
tapeworm has answers

we romanced in Bonn
I spoke what German I knew
—danke schoen, darling!

paper gashed and crimped
jagged scrawls engraved with rage
no haiku today

ill-written romance—
promises inked with kisses
taste just like fiction

charming sunny day
strolling down the avenue
strange neighbors won't wave

gym remodeling
as an investment venture
sweat equity earned

alarming rooster
crowing at the crack of dawn
cock-a-doodle-DON'T!

gone again, enraged
vowing never to return
—I left the light on

flowers soon to be
feathers in the old man's beard
I'm not lichen that

some say clairvoyant
still others say charlatan
all heed the groundhog

vanilla...cherry...
chocolate...rocky road...peach...
holding up the line!

guess I got confused
about nude painting art class
now where are my pants?!

English hamlet pub
question about pentagrams
—keep clear of the moors

Bazooka Joe winks
at Tootsie and Mary Jane
two Hot Tamales!

cinema date night
skeptical first impression
mystery movie

round of whiskey shots
bought for the ladies' table
staggering hubris

two flies on a sink
captive in each other's gaze
two flies, million eyes

glass bubble shattered
on the old gumball machine
rainbow waterfall

not alcoholic,
just have a drinking problem—
two hands and one mouth

over and over
watching *Psycho* all night long
wouldn't hurt a fly

Eve tempted Adam
under a dead apple tree
fruitless fantasy

dandelion breeze
brings a pollenated sneeze
stuffy nose agrees

nudist colony
costume ball invitation
no jacket required

uncork the genie
seeking your every desire
80 proof wishes

drinking pumpkin ale
step one: pour out pumpkin ale
step two: drink real ale

a poet once said
to swim you have to swallow
that man drowned instead

I know all of me
what you get is what you see
you see some of me

bathroom remodel
gold faucets and marble tile
money down the drain

sleepless nights alone
wishing you were here to turn
...off your car alarm!

tears stream down my face
wishing you never returned
pollen season strikes

vanilla cone scoop
plopped on the scorching sidewalk
army ant jackpot

teen riot ensued
Kardashians or *RuPaul?!*
—dad took the remote

record profits at
the dynamite factory
business is booming!

shiny new sailboat
cruising through the marina
fishing compliments

Might dear Watson find
Sherlock Holmes at Scotland Yard?
—Elementary!

SECTION III
TANKA

I hope you enjoyed my haiku and senryu. However, the time spent reading the three-line poems in this book has come to an end as we move on to explore tanka.

What is Tanka?

While tanka may initially appear as an extension of haiku, they hold a distinct charm and depth that sets them apart.

Compared to the common three-line, 5-7-5 syllable pattern description of traditional haiku, tanka are composed of five lines in a 5-7-5-7-7 syllable pattern with a total of 31 syllables. However, as with haiku, the Japanese phonetic units, which compare to syllables, are typically mismatched in translation from language to language. Contemporary tanka are often written without regard for syllable counts, opting for a direct and concise writing approach similar to haiku.

Love Me Tomorrow

While haiku dates back about 300 years, tanka traces its origins nearly 1,200 years ago to Japan's 9th-century Heian Period. When people of the era were courting, on the day after a date, the suitor would compose a tanka and send it to his love interest as a "love letter" of sorts, writing of his thoughts on their time spent together. He, in turn, could expect a reply in kind—that is, if all went well on their date.

The traditional purpose of the tanka is to express emotions and personal reflection, though its style has undergone many changes over the centuries. While contemporary tanka may cover any subject, they still follow established guidelines.

One Good Turn

Tanka consists of two parts:

1. The upper three lines of the tanka (*kami no ku*) describe an image, scene, setting or experience.
2. The lower two lines of the tanka (*shimo no ku*) express the author's feelings or thoughts on the poem's first part, often comparing them using a tangible element, metaphor or analogy.

A turn, or pivot, connects the two parts, most often occurring in the third line, comprised of a word or expression that changes the tone or perception of the first half while also relating to the second half of the tanka, bringing synergy to the poem. This turn is a crucial element of tanka, as it often introduces a new perspective or layer of meaning, enhancing the poem's emotional impact. In this way, tanka has a juxtapositional aspect similar to that of haiku, that of something tangible paired with a reflection or emotion to complete the poem.

When combining these elements, a well-crafted tanka should flow as one sentence or thought. The reader should be able to visualize the subject, get a sense of the turn, and then interpret the reflection as to how it connects to the subject in one smooth sequence with deep meaning or intention. You will get a feel for this as you read my tanka through this book section.

These tanka are written following a 5-7-5-7-7 pattern, some with a "love letter" theme. I hope that by sharing them with you, you will gain an appreciation for the form and its potential for personal expression.

deny my desire
I dared hallucinate love
so intense I wept
flames fed me, ashes bled me
never you, only dreams of you

echo of my touch
our supple dance with deft grace
coaxes my caress
sonic language a sweet song
the blurred road beckons us on

autumn's fallen veil
jutting through a snow-covered
pathway underfoot
crisp crackle of brittle leaves
trekking through winter's glory

heavenly garden
hush of a serpent's whisper
seducing with sin
purity graces virtue
depravity covets vice

sipping black coffee
alive to a wildwood scene
peering through windows
am I nature's voyeur or
do stoic trees behold me?

to defend one's heart
in a harbor of refuge
free of life's laments
you invite nothing less than
perfect disaster

heaven crowns the grace
of solace to stranded souls
blessed by the divine
angel tears flow down my cheeks
yours shed, forever now mine

time lost to the past
weaves a stubborn crown of thorns
wrath of endless grief
how blessed are we when we choose
to live in the wondrous now

forgotten byway
silent as a mystery
through murky wildwoods
I spend time lost in my mind
where I find myself within

lost to the degree
of rewinding memories
decaying each day
looking for my reflection
in shadows of what we were

seductive black rose

lures sinful fascination

and dark temptation

though petals may wilt and fall

its thorns remain forever

ivory pages

lavished with gilt-edge wisdom

spilled in sanguine ink

priceless words to consume

in tomes of ageless genius

idled in a field
lost in peaceful reflection
of a long journey
each mile a traveler walks
with still a lifetime to go

opalescent stars
pinning indigo moonlight
to the nighttime sky
hardly can such dark beauty
evoke dreams of sunshine days

lissome silhouette

shaping a heaven on earth

I yearn to possess

just a dreamer from afar

seen and unseen in your eyes

souls of the poets

wield breathtaking flair etching

emotion in words

sacred gifts of creation

freeing us to touch the stars

elegant duet
mirrored on a placid lake
of sunrise shimmer
swans the resplendent jewels
crowning with exquisite grace

shadowed by tall trees
on a vast sunny meadow
lulled by spring breezes
magnificent wild poppies
dwarf the scene with utmost charm

mountain reflection
told on a sleepy river
under an old bridge
wary not to wake this scene
wandering from dream to dream

pick axe and shovel
clawing at hidden treasure
salting fertile ground
lovely roses bloomed in soil
where cold graves have been dug

sea shanties echo
fortunes and maidens of lore
spun in turning tides
wanderlusts long forsaken
fated by fickle swan roads

darkly sweet angel
cloaked in a morbid shadow
of wintry despair
she takes strange comfort in cold
wishing only for black snow

watercolor clouds
portrayed your angelic face
soft drops kissed my cheeks
I folded my umbrella
letting love rain over me

your mystic presence
lingers from the touch of skin
to depths of my core
would that I could breathe you in
and hold you forevermore

movie scenes of us
soda sips and popcorn crunch
now just memories
happily ever after
replayed again and again

patchwork clouds linger
trees blur dim lit horizons
bits of me scattered
combing miles of memories
piecing puzzles whole again

antique photographs
of people I've never known
places never seen
curled in shapes without shape names
like the nameless faces shown

seeking directions
to sentimental journeys
not found on a map
familiar highways traveled
to unknown destinations

your eyes are raw stars

ravishing my galaxy

dazzling in darkness

I climb the sky to heaven

mantled in sweetest stardust

walking together

where our lonely hearts crumbled

collecting rubble

with bricks of our broken selves

we build a castle for two

SECTION IV
HAIBUN

Welcome to the final section of this book, poised to explore haibun, a form of poetry that I've grown quite fond of.

Haibun originated in 17th-century Japan from legendary poet Matsuo Basho; however, the first English-language haibun appeared in the early 1960s, making it a comparatively new short-form writing style.

Put simply, haibun is a blend of prose and haiku poetry. Each element relies on its strengths to work together while remaining independent, simultaneously contrasting and complementing each other. The distinctive mix of these elements combine to weave a rich tapestry of writing to create a powerful haibun.

While haibun does have some common guidelines and suggestions directing its form, it also offers a wide range of creative freedom, allowing for individual interpretation and expression. This introduction aims to equip you with enough knowledge to appreciate and enjoy the haibun I've published in this book.

Prose: Show Me, Don't Tell Me

Haibun prose often describes a scene, character, event or memorable moment but can be about anything, whether fact-based or fictitious. The prose of haibun is usually written in the present tense to provide a sense of "being there" for the reader, but it can also be a second, or third-person narrative.

A haibun's prose should employ powerful, descriptive, evocative and concise writing colored with vivid imagery. It should draw readers in, compelling them to learn more about its story. Writers should include only necessary wording without redundancy.

Most importantly, the prose should only show, not tell, leaving the reader to interpret the haibun uniquely and draw conclusions about its meaning.

Haiku: Fuel for the Fire

Haiku are integral in creating well-written haibun. Without good haiku, no amount of brilliant prose will allow for haibun to succeed. For this reason, haiku are generally created first before setting out to write prose for haibun.

Haiku adds to or enhances the meaning of the prose, offering a reflection or complementary quality to the subject or theme and often including a sharp juxtaposed quality. As in the case of prose, haiku adopts a "show, don't tell" approach, leaving the reader to his own interpretation. In this way, creating effective interaction between the prose and haiku leads to the sum of both becoming a greater, more compelling haibun.

The Title: Use It, Don't Lose It

Unlike haiku and tanka, haibun include titles. A title provides the writer with another component to add a compelling descriptive element to the haibun that can interact with the prose and haiku to augment the reader's impression of the haibun. Again, the title should show, not tell, and be as innovative as the prose and haiku. If you're writing a haibun about red roses, the last thing you want for a title is "Red Roses." Haibun should always take advantage of the creative opportunity for enhancement by utilizing an intriguing or imaginative title.

A Final Word on Haibun

I enjoy combining my passion for haiku and creative writing to compose haibun. I like to think of the prose as drawing readers into the story, painting a picture that leads you curiously further and further in before the haiku strikes like a lightning bolt.

When I write a haibun, I always have an idea of what I'm writing about, but if crafted correctly, that idea will always be a mystery to everyone else. There is always more than one way to interpret my haibun, and in some cases, many ways to interpret them.

And that is the beauty of haibun—they exist to entertain, provoke thought and reveal meaning according to each reader in their own way.

Enchanting Rose

precious flower
scent of a rose
on cold winds

I was summoned to an old brick apartment building where countless lives had been lived in the city over some 80 years or more. The one I was there for was a young woman who failed to show up for work that morning. In fact, she hadn't been seen in days. A coworker called—not family, not a best friend, not a lover. He was a friend, anyway, as evident by the concern shaping his face. Where was she?

In the hall, outside her door...I knew. With the landlord's key, I entered alone.

Clues were there to be found. A calendar filled with doctor appointments. A dozen prescription medications, perhaps a dozen too many for someone so young. They were stacked in a kitchen cabinet decorated with photographs of her smiling with children, possibly nephews and nieces, surrounded by pictures of dreamy nature scenes and inspirational quotes taped to the walls.

Her vibrant spirit echoed in her footprints. I followed their trail, looking for a photograph of her with a special someone, or perhaps a vase of red roses, or a card written with romance. Sadly, there were none. Only a puzzle missing a piece or two, left incomplete.

beautiful flower
priceless rose
treasured by few

Trick of the Light

The calm serenity of the day belied the river current unseen. He crossed the ice many times, yet one step, at last, cracked an evil smile. A spiderweb fanned out with absurd speed and a staccato howl. Shelves collapsed, fingers clawed, and panic screamed. The smile turned voracious maw, devouring him as he narrowed at the sight of his vanishing light.

twist of fate
living a daydream
nightmare

Cortland Avenue

I stood atop spiral stairs, awash in hysteria, deflecting arrows of blame for a lifetime of poor choices bleeding out long before my arrival. I have seen misery, inhaled the scent of carnage, listened to all manner of anguished cries. Yet, I had never seen *you* until that moment.

Descending those twisting stairs and turning, there you were, a mesmerizing shadow in empty eyes. For that fleeting moment, it seemed as though you compelled those eyes to look up and lock onto mine. I understood that we would meet again, but no longer as strangers.

roll the dice
snake eyes
watching you

Sketch a Little Magic

One of my favorite childhood possessions was Crayola crayons—the big box with 64 colors. That box always let my imagination soar to whatever worlds I wanted to go. The scent of the crayons was heavenly, a scent that embodied the very essence of color itself.

I always felt sorry for my friends who had the box of 32 colors, or worse. I didn't even know there were boxes that only had 8 colors. My coloring books were so much more vivid than theirs, but it was difficult to share mine since they were the only colors I had. I feared I might lose them forever.

I still carry those crayons. Now, when I see someone who looks like they could use a little Sky Blue or Cornflower, or even favorites like Silver or Gold, I'm always eager to share. I know they never had the big box when I show them colors they've never seen before.

torn paper
in shades of gray...
a rainbow!

Dark Mistress

From the moment I wake, you're all I desire. I know you're near, waiting, knowing I crave you like a sensuous addiction. Your intoxicating scent lingers in the air, enticing me closer. One kiss is all it takes to surrender to your seduction. I savor all of you as I'm bathed in ecstasy, powerless against the magic of your potion coursing through my veins. You ignite my lust for more, but more is never enough. I'm yours, now and forevermore.

tasting your essence
rich and sweet like
cream and sugar

Decaying Orbit

He would come at various times, both day and evening, but never after dark. His mother would not allow it. Always wanting a cigarette, often with nervous desperation. If you wanted small talk, you would have to delay giving him one because he didn't care to chat. He just wanted to smoke, and quick, before *Matlock* started. Or before his mother found out. She must have known, with him coming home reeking of tobacco, yet she never said a word to me. I only saw her once, the quintessential little old lady standing on the sidewalk, dwarfed in his shadow, which is how I learned they lived next door. She was the world, he the spinning moon, and Andy Griffith was waiting.

butts in the gutter
drama in the parlor
toys in the attic

Moving Picture

Fog would have been nice. With the warmth of this lovely day crashing into the chilly night you'd expect the scene would be flawless, but no. It's just cold tonight. Too cold and too late for most. Yet here we are, as it was written in the stars, the cast assembled and ready. Splendid, and your silhouette in the moonlight is utterly captivating. Exactly as imagined.

The script can be forgotten now. It's all method from here.

blood moon...
I've been waiting
all your life

Quicksand Inertia

I'm not entirely sure what a fickle wind is, but I suppose the sense of melancholy anchoring me on a sunny day fits the description. I know I'll be okay since I always am when it happens; I just don't know when it will happen, and that's what makes it fickle, I guess.

Or maybe it's about the wind, not the melancholy.

On second thought, no. Now that I think about it, whether I'm indoors or outside doesn't seem to matter. Yes, the more I ponder, the more I'm convinced fickle isn't about the wind.

In fact, there really is no wind. Just melancholy and sun.

infinite stars
losing count
every night

Mid-Century Modern

She ruminated years of presents on coffee tables and under trees, destined for happy hands. Mountains of twisted ribbon and flashy tattered paper long since laid to rest in forgotten landfills. The dogged pressure to top last year and the year before. She knows the neighbors, and they're always watching.

Sitting by the fireplace in her husband's beloved naugahyde chair, a split in the cushion reminded her that nothing lasts forever. She slipped a finger into the vinyl and felt the dreamy padding, wondering what she might be able to hide in there.

three ruby taps
her own tornado
still spinning

Our Morning Tea[1]

I'm awakened again by the quietest silence tapping my shoulder. Gliding into the kitchen dumbstruck as a marionette on a darkened stage, bright lights spotting my rendered smile, I'm uncertain what moves me even as I'm transported.

Poured cream swirls in black tea from a spoon clinking on thin china cups. The same thin cups you always said tea tastes best in. An empty cup rests on a saucer across the table from me. I brewed more tea than I should have again.

routines without you
are hollow madness
my strings are broken

Observing our home, I notice things I now realize were always here. Sparrows chirping in the garden. A ticking grandfather clock. Floral wallpaper you hated. Your favorite pillow creased on the daybed. That noisy spoon. I suppose I'll keep noticing these things as time rattles downstream. The river never waits.

Our spaniel goes about her usual business of being a pleasant dog. Unaffected, or so it would seem. I wonder. I might feel envy, but I feel nothing.

coldest of winters
eternity burns
longer than forever

Endnotes

1. "Our Morning Tea" was first published in the *Scarlet Dragonfly Journal*—April 2024.

Acknowledgements

This book is the culmination of a lifelong goal to become a published author. From inception to completion, my wife, Hollie, has been there for me, eager to help, advise and support. Her meticulous attention to detail in the book's layout and insightful editing suggestions have significantly enhanced the final product. She is more than a match for my attention to detail and a fantastic ally to have in my corner. This book would not be the same without her.

The writing community has been a catalyst for accelerating my growth. The interactions I've had with fellow writers and poets have helped shape my writing style and approach. I appreciate every writer and poet who bravely shares their innermost thoughts and feelings, inviting scrutiny and criticism. Your courage is inspiring.

Last but not least, I thank you, the reader of my book. Your time is valuable, so spending some of it reading my work is perhaps the greatest compliment I could receive. You have my most sincere gratitude.

If you enjoyed my poetry, please consider rating this book or submitting a review from where you purchased it.

Thank you!

About the Author

Leon Tefft is a writer, poet and author of *Haiku Traditions*.

Born and raised in Chicago, Illinois, Leon's love of poetry originated with the first haiku he wrote as a teenager, spurring decades of creative writing expressed though poetry and short story fiction. His poetry has appeared in numerous online and print publications. He is a member of the Haiku Society of America and the Tanka Society of America.

Leon draws inspiration for his creativity from a wide range of unique experiences throughout his life. His resume includes writer, artist, actor, celebrity bodyguard, trader and business owner. He is an avid reader with noted interests in history, philosophy and photography.

Leon is a retired police officer with 30 years of distinguished service to his hometown City of Chicago. He currently resides in South Carolina with his wife, Hollie.